To Dr. Antígona Segura Peralta, Astrobiologist, [...] Astrobiologist, NASA. The fact-checking and p[...] [...]us scientists like you make The Science Starters Collection possible.

Notes for Teachers & Parents

Effortlessly teach science to children as you rhyme your way through various scientific fields. The rhyming narrative employed by The Science Starters Collection engages children's curiosity, makes learning fun, promotes memory retention, and helps improve reading, spelling, and writing skills. Technical language is used throughout each book to widen children's vocabulary and to inspire questions. For the questions that arise, the science behind the rhymes is explained in further detail, either alongside the text or in the back of the book.

Creating a diverse set of role models that children can relate to is at the core of The Science Starters Collection. By reading these books in classrooms, or at home, you foster a passion for science and introduce children to the things they, and others, can do. Guide children into their desired field of science by referring to the Becoming a Scientist page at the back of each book.

Fact-checked by:
Dr. Antígona Segura Peralta, Astrobiologist, UNAM
Dr. Giada Arney, Astrobiologist, NASA

Illustrated by:
Brettany Frederick

Page Layout by:
Chase Nuttall

ISBN: 978-0-9981541-1-4

Astrobiologist Aurora
Searches for Life in Outer Space

Autumn Lorraine, Author & Scientist
Illustrated by Brettany Frederick

Autumn Lorraine Publishing

Have you ever wondered if
we're all alone . . .
If Earth is the only planet
where life has grown?

I ponder this question
more often than most,
So I spend my time
looking for another
biological host.

To understand big
words like *biological host*
I like to think about what
each word means.

Host is another word for *place*
and *biological* is another
word for *life.*

So a biological host is
a place with life.

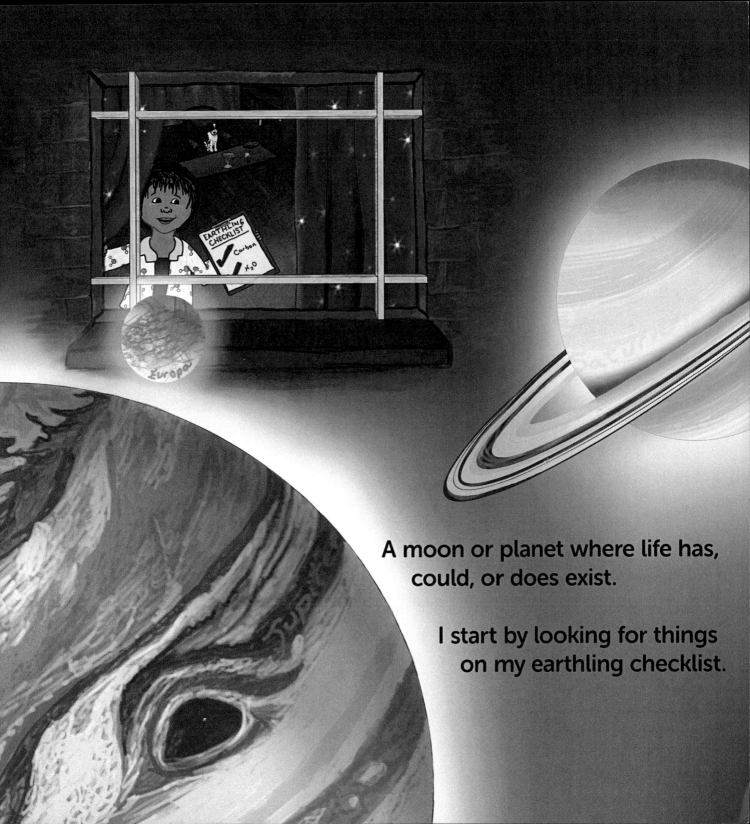

A moon or planet where life has, could, or does exist.

I start by looking for things on my earthling checklist.

Carbon is an element made within stars, and it serves as the primary building block of life's genetic code.

All earthlings need carbon and H_2O.

With these two ingredients, tiny and massive life can grow.

A genetic code is the language of life.

Just like letters string together to form a word, and words string together to form a sentence, and sentences string together to form a story, elements string together to form molecules, molecules string together to form genes, and genes string together to form the genetic code.

H_2O is water. The H stands for hydrogen, the first element created during the Big Bang, and the O stands for oxygen. Water provides the environment for the chemistry of life to occur. Hydrogen, oxygen, and carbon, the three elements on our earthling checklist, are some of the most common elements in the universe.

A common genetic code is shared by all life, varying from species to species by only a tiny amount. For instance, we are 99.9% genetically identical to each other and 99% genetically identical to chimpanzees!

From microbes, Earth's most ancient creatures,

To plants and mammals with a diversity of features.

Microbes were the first earthlings to form, over 3.5 billion years ago. Thousands of them clumped together are smaller than the tip of a pen. In fact, there are millions of them spread out on your skin right now!

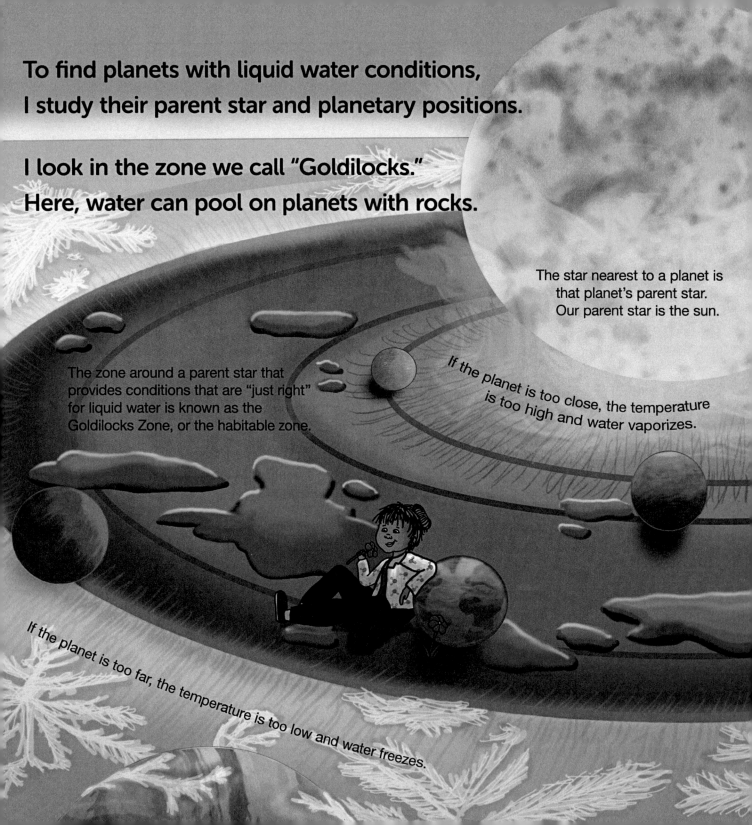

To find planets with liquid water conditions,
I study their parent star and planetary positions.

I look in the zone we call "Goldilocks."
Here, water can pool on planets with rocks.

The star nearest to a planet is that planet's parent star. Our parent star is the sun.

The zone around a parent star that provides conditions that are "just right" for liquid water is known as the Goldilocks Zone, or the habitable zone.

If the planet is too close, the temperature is too high and water vaporizes.

If the planet is too far, the temperature is too low and water freezes.

Proxima Centauri

Proxima b

GOLDILOCKS

The closest Goldilocks planet
is Proxima Centauri b.
It orbits our neighbor star,
Proxima Centauri.

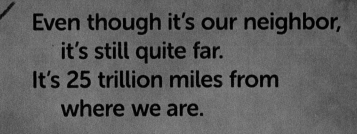

25,000,000,000,000 miles!

Even though it's our neighbor,
it's still quite far.
It's 25 trillion miles from
where we are.

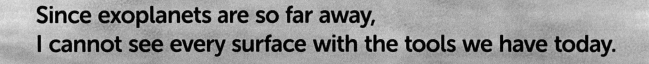

Since exoplanets are so far away,
I cannot see every surface with the tools we have today.

But their shadows let me know how big
    and where they are
As they pass in front of their parent star.

LIGHT

TIME

Exoplanets are planets that orbit other suns.

A decrease in light lets us know
that something, like a planet,
is blocking the star's light and casting
a shadow on our detectors.

Coronagraphs and starshades are space tools being developed right now. Each of them is designed to block the overwhelming glare of stars, allowing us to see the planets previously hidden by bright light.

You can do something similar with your hand. If you notice something in the sky that you have trouble seeing because of the sunlight, you can use your hand to block the sun's glare.

When you become an astrobiologist, you'll have much better tools.

Like coronagraphs and starshades that help photogragh planets' watery pools.

They'll do so by reducing the parent star's blinding effect,

Allowing us to see things more clear and direct.

The illustration above shows a starshade - a paper-thin screen about the size of a baseball diamond floating thousands of miles in front of the trailing telescope.

The massive size of the starshade and the distance between it and the telescope create a low-light environment for the telescope's camera to photograph whatever may be orbiting the star.

Until then, I'll teach you what we've come to know:

There are thousands of known exoplanets, and that number continues to grow!

The first exoplanet discovered was 51 Pegasi b.
It was found because its parent star is quite wobbly.

The wobble of a star lets us know a planet is near,
Tugging on the star as it orbits once per year.

As a planet moves in front of a star from our perspective, the star tilts toward the planet and towards us due to the planet's gravitational force.

As a planet moves behind the star from our perspective, its gravitational force tugs the star backward and away from us. Since planets move around stars on an oval-like path, they get close, then far, then close, then far, forcing the star to wobble back and forth, which produces a signal in the light we see.

A year is defined by how many days it takes for a planet to orbit its parent star one time. It takes Earth 365 days to orbit our sun. 51 Pegasi b orbits its sun in just four days!

Finding 51 Pegasi b was a scientific
    breakthrough . . .

It proved that our solar system is
    one of at least two.

Since then, we've discovered thousands more,
And our space-based telescopes continue to explore!

A solar system is what we call a star
and the objects that move around it.
Our solar system is a star that is orbited
by eight planets and over 100 moons, plus
comets, asteroids, and other cool space stuff.

Of these thousands, our solar system is the most understood,
And I hope the chances of finding life within it are pretty good.

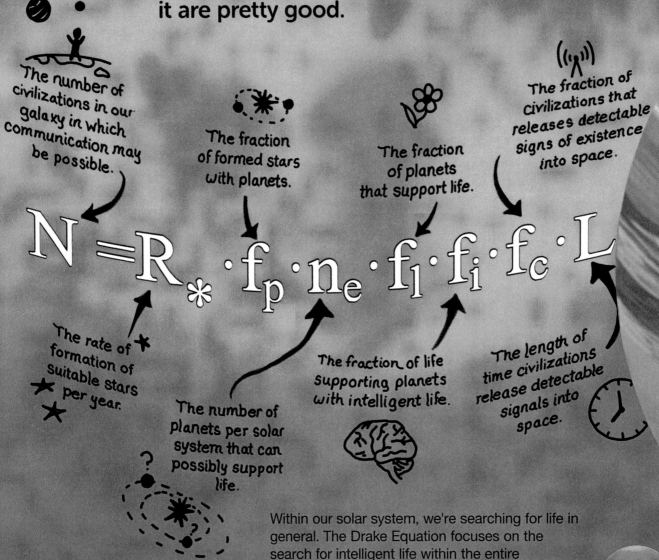

The number of civilizations in our galaxy in which communication may be possible.

The fraction of formed stars with planets.

The fraction of planets that support life.

The fraction of civilizations that releases detectable signs of existence into space.

$$N = R_* \cdot f_p \cdot n_e \cdot f_l \cdot f_i \cdot f_c \cdot L$$

The rate of formation of suitable stars per year.

The number of planets per solar system that can possibly support life.

The fraction of life supporting planets with intelligent life.

The length of time civilizations release detectable signals into space.

Within our solar system, we're searching for life in general. The Drake Equation focuses on the search for intelligent life within the entire Milky Way Galaxy, not just our solar system.

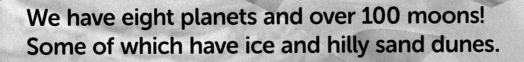

We have eight planets and over 100 moons!
Some of which have ice and hilly sand dunes.

Planet

Moon

Sun

The difference between a moon and
a planet is what the object orbits.
A moon orbits a planet and a planet
orbits a star.

Mars has both, so it's a planet that we study.
We want to know if in between the ice and
sand, it's muddy.

**Photos of Mars revealed evidence of water
So NASA deployed Curiosity,
   a robotic Mars trotter.**

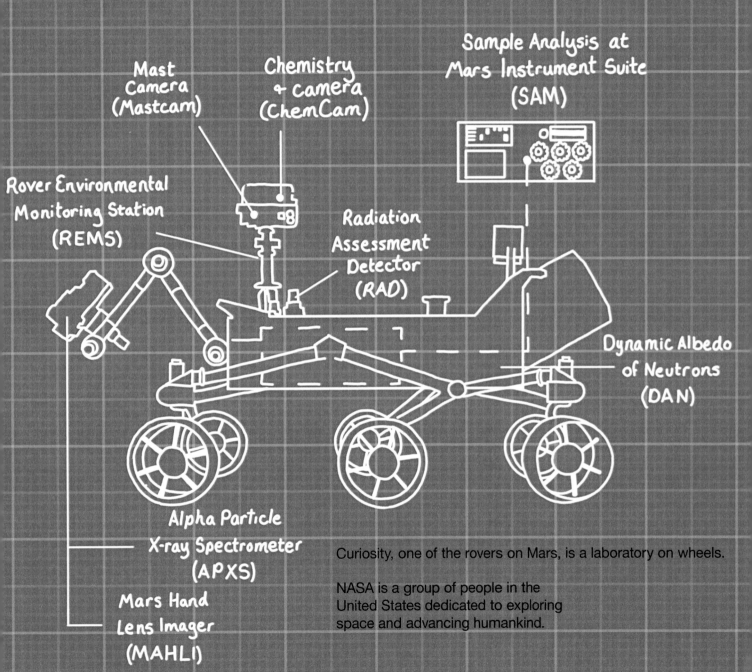

Sample Analysis at
Mars Instrument Suite
(SAM)

Mast
Camera
(Mastcam)

Chemistry
& camera
(ChemCam)

Rover Environmental
Monitoring Station
(REMS)

Radiation
Assessment
Detector
(RAD)

Dynamic Albedo
of Neutrons
(DAN)

Alpha Particle
X-ray Spectrometer
(APXS)

Mars Hand
Lens Imager
(MAHLI)

Curiosity, one of the rovers on Mars, is a laboratory on wheels.

NASA is a group of people in the
United States dedicated to exploring
space and advancing humankind.

It's looking for molecules that are carbon-based
By sampling rocks and soil most likely to have a trace.

Curiosity has been cruising around on the surface of Mars taking pictures and samples of stuff like rocks and soil to determine if Mars has ever supported life. You can view the photos taken by Curiosity on NASA's website.

Another location of interest is Titan,
a moon of Saturn.

It looks like Earth and follows a
seasonal pattern.

Titan has clouds, lakes, and even oceans!
But they're made of very different chemical potions.

On Titan, natural gas is liquid in form
And it pours from the clouds during
every rainstorm.

On Earth, natural gas is a gas because of how warm Earth is. As temperatures cool, the natural gas molecules lose energy and get closer together forming a liquid. The temperature on Titan's surface is about -290 degrees Fahrenheit. That's definitely cold enough to turn natural gas into liquid. If you watch water boil, you can watch a similar process occur in reverse. As the water heats, the water molecules gain energy and move apart from each other, producing steam.

So Titan is too cold for our type of life,
But another may flourish there without any strife.

Jupiter's moon Europa is a
little more inviting

Because recently, there was
a water plume sighting.

A water plume is like
a volcano, except water,
instead of lava, erupts from the
top. The suspected water
plumes, photographed by the Hubble Space Telescope,
rose over 100 miles above the icy surface of Europa.

The evidence suggests that water is what we saw.
If we confirm this, it will be a moment of
excitement and awe.

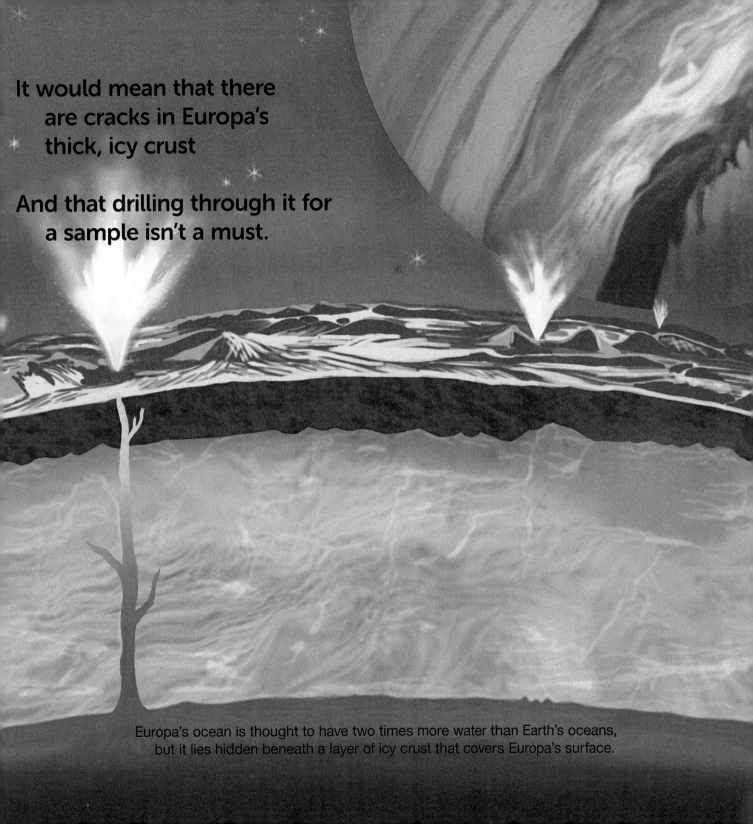

It would mean that there are cracks in Europa's thick, icy crust

And that drilling through it for a sample isn't a must.

Europa's ocean is thought to have two times more water than Earth's oceans, but it lies hidden beneath a layer of icy crust that covers Europa's surface.

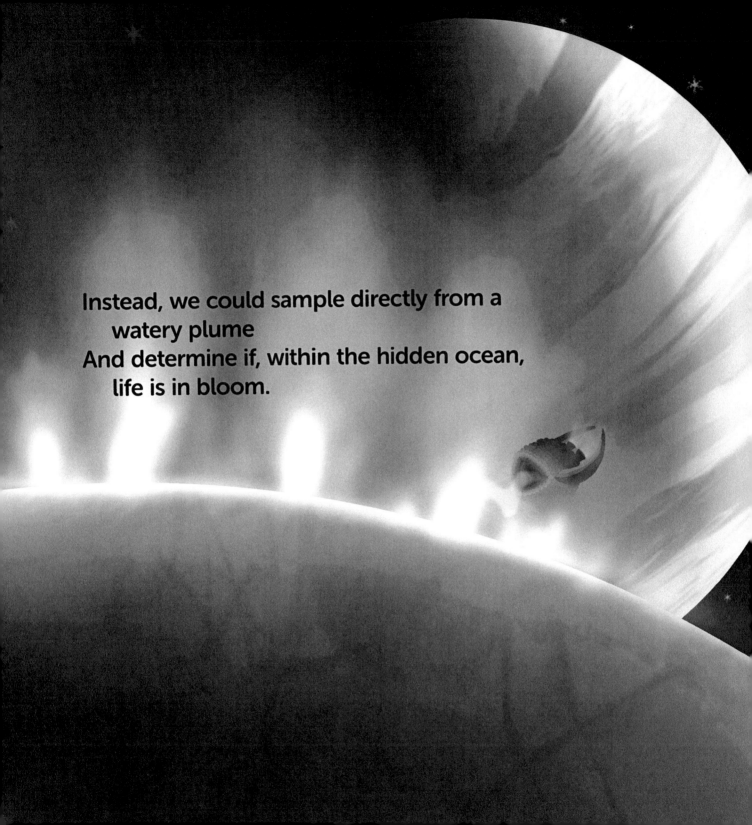

Instead, we could sample directly from a watery plume
And determine if, within the hidden ocean, life is in bloom.

I'm excited for our future and the knowledge we'll gain!
Especially since every time I learn, I strengthen my brain!

Your brain is stronger now too!
You've learned so much that you're a
newer, smarter version of you!

I Know I Can, But How?

Dr. Antígona Segura Peralta's path to becoming Mexico's first female astrobiologist.

I read my dad's science fiction books when I was a little girl
And my mom bought me astronomy books that made my imagination swirl

I loved the stars, and all life too
So when I thought of studying just one, I didn't know what to do.

Then "Cosmos" by Carl Sagan aired on TV
And it was like he was talking directly to me.

He told me about the search for life in outer space
And I couldn't stop myself from dancing in place.

My two favorite things combined into one
My quest to figure out what I'd become was finally done!

Then I learned that astrobiology was unheard of in my town
And I felt my dreams begin to drown.

I was lost for a while, and I didn't know what to do
So after high school I studied physics hoping to find a clue.

The clue didn't come until I finished my master's degree,
When I found the only astrobiologist in my country.

He, Dr. Rafael Navarro-Gonzalez, became my advisor
And while working with him and Dr. Jim Kasting, I became a bit wiser.

I did experiments to learn if life evolved on Mars
And then, I started looking for life around other stars!

Soon after, I realized that the confused little girl I used to be
Is now a grown woman studying astrobiology!

"Now, it is easier to become an astrobiologist. NASA has the Institute of Astrobiology with lots of interesting research programs where scientist from all kinds of backgrounds can work to understand life as a universal phenomenon. Several universities, like Penn State and Washington University, have graduate programs where you can learn all you need to become an astrobiologist."
— Dr. Antígona Segura Peralta, Astrobiologist, Universidad Nacional Autónoma de México

Becoming an Astrobiologist

What is an astrobiologist's typical day like?
It depends on the type of astrobiologist you are. Some spend their days collecting samples and analyzing them in the laboratory, whereas others run computer simulations to understand the types of planetary environments that may be able to support life and how to recognize them on exoplanets. All of them though, spend a lot of time thinking, reading, writing, using computers, and doing math. These tasks are tools they use to analyze data and to write papers explaining what they've learned. Experienced astrobiologists may also teach classes, manage teams of researchers, and help develop future plans for NASA. The everyday efforts of an astrobiologist are aimed at answering a question we've been asking for hundreds of years: Are we alone in the universe?

How can I become an astrobiologist?
Below are a few guidelines to help you on your journey:
• Learn and develop a passion for math, the language of the universe. Learning a new language is challenging, but you learned one, which means you can learn another.
• Take a variety of science classes throughout junior high, high school, and college. Find the type of science that interests you the most and think about how you can relate it to astrobiology.
• Actively participate in your local astronomy society and other science based groups that interest you.
• Regularly visit NASA's website to keep current with space news.
• Receive a bachelor of science degree in a science like biology, math, chemistry, geology, astronomy, physics, earth science, ecology, oceanography, zoology, volcanology, or botany.
• Keep in mind that your professors are one of your greatest resources. They may seem boring or intimidating, but don't let that stop you from developing a professional relationship with them. Attend their office hours, ask them questions, and learn about the path they took to become who they are today.
• Work or volunteer as a research assistant in a lab studying things that interest you while obtaining your bachelor's degree.
• Answer this question: What questions must I answer? Then earn a PhD in a scientific field that will allow you to answer those questions.

"Know that you don't have to do it all. Become an expert in one field, tackle a question relevant to astrobiology in that field, and seek feedback from experts in other fields. Most importantly, always stay curious and excited about the universe we live in!"
—Dr. Giada Arney, Astrobiologist, NASA

About the Author

In a world full of stereotypes, Autumn struggled to overcome hers. She thought she could do things that others said she couldn't, she felt she belonged in environments that others tried to keep her out of, and she didn't have any relatable role models in her fields of interest. The Science Starters Series is Autumn's attempt to help children overcome their struggles by introducing them to the things they, and others, can do while providing them with role models they can relate to.

Where science is concerned, Autumn is what you'd call an early adopter. She was just four when she started analyzing bugs and tuning in to Bill Nye the Science Guy. Twelve years into her career in the sciences, she began writing to foster that passion in the next generation of young explorers.

Before becoming a writer, Autumn obtained a formal education in biochemistry and women and gender studies while working in the pharmaceutical industry. In her late twenties she entered the biotechnology industry and academia.

Today, she assists in the management of the biochemistry and chemistry teaching labs at her local university. In her free time, she attends various science classes, writes The Science Starters Series, and explores the awe-inspiring state of Oregon.

About the Illustrator

Dreams of becoming an animator led Brettany out of her small hometown. While studying media, advertising, and digital art, she also pursued her growing interest in science. As she simultaneously studied these seemingly different subjects, Brettany realized that they go hand in hand.

With artistic talent already flowing through her genes, she focused her efforts on science. She delved into the fascinating and challenging world of human anatomy, physiology, biology and chemistry while working as a laboratory assistant in the chemistry teaching labs. This is where she met Autumn Lorraine.

Brettany's talents, unique perspectives, and bubbly personality quickly caught Autumn's attention and the two began working together outside of the lab. Illustrating Astrobiologist Aurora allowed Brettany to act upon her philosophy that science needs art to be understood and to flourish in the minds of its students.

Currently, Brettany can be found studying, endlessly laughing through the struggle with her phenomenal friends, and walking her miniature Australian shepherd, Berry Buttons.